SCHOLASTIC

Graphic Organizers for the Overhead: Reading and Writing

BY JENNIFER JACOBSON

NEW YORK • TORONTO • LONDON • AUCKLAND • SYDNEY
MEXICO CITY • NEW DELHI • HONG KONG • BUENOS AIRES

Teaching *Resources*

Acknowledgments

Many thanks to Liza Charlesworth and Danielle Blood.

For information about Jennifer Jacobson's staff development programs, please visit her website at
www.jenniferjacobson.com.

....

Cover design by Brian LaRossa
Cover and interior illustrations by Teresa Anderko
Interior design by Sydney Wright
Teacher pages edited by Shoshana Wolfe

ISBN-10: 0-439-60971-2
ISBN-13: 978-0-439-60971-5

Published by Scholastic Inc.
Produced by becker&mayer! for Scholastic Inc.
All rights reserved.
Printed and assembled in China.

1 2 3 4 5 6 7 8 9 10 14 13 12 11 10 09 08 07

Contents

Reading

Writing

Vocabulary and Word Choice

Flexible Use

Introduction

Welcome to *Graphic Organizers for the Overhead: Reading and Writing*! Designed for flexible use, these 25 graphic organizers for the overhead boost key reading and writing skills. First, use the transparency for a whole-group lesson; then provide students with the reproducible version for independent use. These activities and graphic organizers are perfect for trait-based writing, responding to fiction and nonfiction, making connections to text, building vocabulary, and more.

What Is a Graphic Organizer?

A graphic organizer is a visual representation of information that reveals relationships between facts, concepts, or ideas. Graphic organizers provide schemata: a way of structuring information or arranging key concepts into a pattern using labels (Bromley et al., 1995). Charts, diagrams, semantic maps, and timelines are all examples of graphic organizers designed to help students configure (or reconfigure) information so that comprehension of content and understanding of learning strategies increases.

Why Use Graphic Organizers in the Classroom?

Graphic organizers offer a means for determining what students know, what they need to know (including any misconceptions they might harbor), and what they retain after a learning activity. Graphic organizers offer students an efficient way to direct their attention, record key information, display their thinking (which is often more creative or divergent when using a graphic organizer), and monitor their use of learning strategies. No doubt visual learners benefit from the use of graphic organizers, but when graphic organizers are used as a focal activity with groups (particularly with the use of an overhead transparency), auditory learners benefit from this practice as well. Graphic organizers also help bilingual students convert complex content into manageable chunks and students with learning disabilities organize verbal information, thereby improving their recall of the content (Kim et al., 2004).

Putting Research Into Practice

Research has demonstrated that graphic organizers help students to:

▹ connect prior knowledge to new information (Guastello, 2000).

▹ integrate language and thinking in an organized format (Bromley et al., 1995).

▹ increase comprehension and retention of text (Boyle and Weishaar, 1997; Change, K. et al., 2002; Moore and Readence, 1984).

▹ organize writing (Ellis, 1994).

▹ engage in mid- to high-level thinking along Bloom's Taxonomy (application, analysis, and synthesis) (Dodge, 2005).

> If the brain can retrieve stored information that is similar to new information, it is more likely to make sense of the new information. This leads to increased understanding and retention (Westwater and Wolf, 2000).

What's Inside This Book?

The 25 graphic organizers are included both as reproducible pages and overhead transparencies. Each comes with a mini-lesson that includes the following sections:

Skills
Notes the skills covered in the activity.

Purpose
Explains the uses and benefits of the activity.

Introducing the Activity
Describes a quick strategy for introducing the activity and piquing students' interest.

Using the Overhead Transparency
Provides step-by-step directions for taking students through the mini-lesson with the overhead transparency. The mini-lesson also serves as an explanation of how students will use the reproducible graphic organizer individually, with partners, or in small groups.

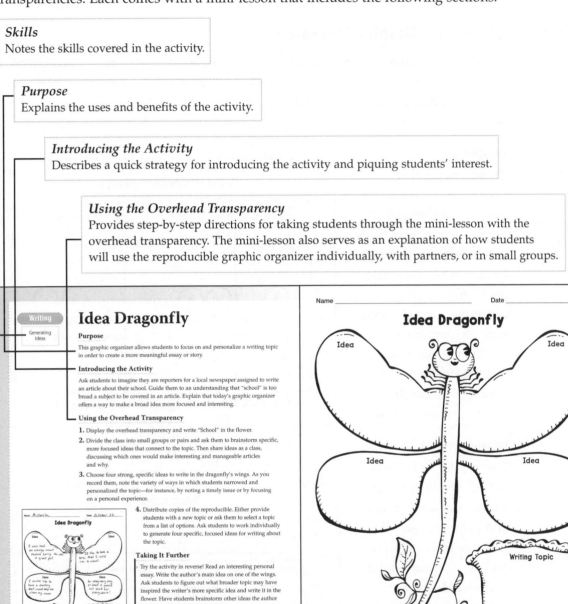

Completed Sample
Shows a sample of the graphic organizer filled in with responses.

Taking It Further
Presents one or two extension activities that either build on the skills and strategies covered in the mini-lesson or use the graphic organizer for a different purpose.

Graphic Organizer
The graphic organizer is presented as a reproducible in the book and as an overhead transparency in the envelope at the back of the book.

How to Use This Book

In selecting an organizer, consider the following:
1. the complexity of the text
2. how the organizer fits the curriculum content
3. how the structural pattern of the text agrees with the organizer selected (Gil-Garcia and Villegas, 2003).

Choosing a Graphic Organizer

The 25 mini-lessons and graphic organizers can be used in any order and adapted as needed. Use the skill matrix on page 9 to find the graphic organizers that best suit your instructional needs. The organizers are organized into four sections by the following topics:

Reading

These five graphic organizers are designed to guide students in responding meaningfully to text they are reading or have read. They help students practice key comprehension strategies such as comparing, predicting, questioning, making inferences, and making text-to-self and text-to-text connections.

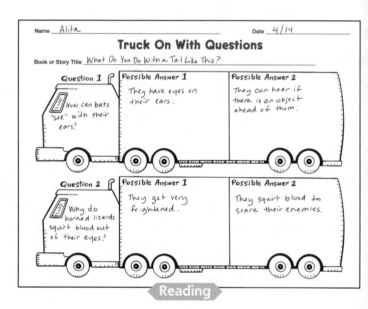

Writing

The graphic organizers in this section are geared toward the writing traits and help students generate ideas, analyze and develop voice, plan and organize their writing, and build sentence fluency. They are designed for different kinds of writing, such as essays, stories, and persuasive writing.

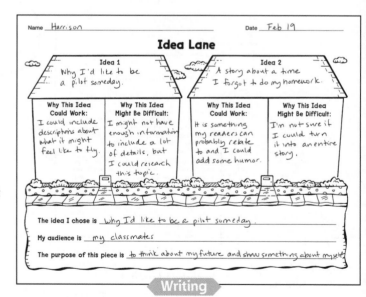

Vocabulary/Word Choice

These four organizers engage students in word study and vocabulary-building activities that will help them as both readers and writers. The activities guide students to see relationships between words and how the same words can be used in different contexts.

Flexible Use

In this section, you'll find graphic organizers that help students recognize the essential connection between reading and writing. Through writing activities, students develop a better understanding of the meaning and construction of texts that they read. When students read and analyze fiction and nonfiction text, they improve their craft as writers as well.

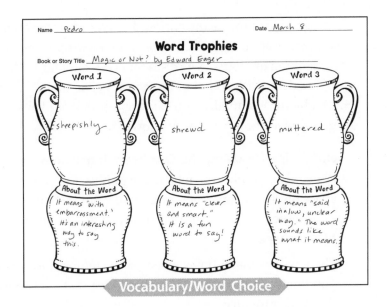

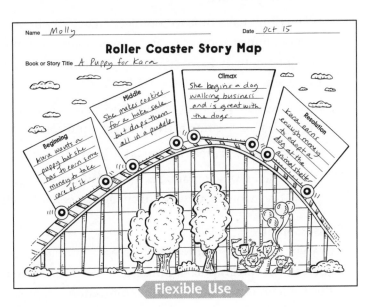

Using the Mini-Lesson and Graphic Organizers

The organizers can be used with the whole class, small groups, or individual students. They are ideal for homework or guiding cooperative learning groups.

Preparation

Before using an organizer, give it a "trial run" to experience the process firsthand. This preparation allows you to see how well the graphic works with the selected text, vocabulary words, or other information being presented. Make any modifications necessary to best meet the needs of your students (Egan, 1999).

Introducing the Graphic Organizer

Research has shown that graphic organizers are most effective when the teacher presents and models the organizer first for the whole group (Bowman et al., 1998).

It is a good idea to use the enclosed overhead transparencies to demonstrate the use of the graphic organizer, pool students' responses, and share critical strategies by "thinking out loud." Once students are familiar with the graphic organizer, provide them with copies of the reproducible to use in small groups, in pairs, or individually. Eventually, you can suggest that students create their own graphic organizers to show what they know. They will enjoy the creative challenge!

Helpful Tips for Using the Overhead Transparencies

▸ Remember, graphic organizers are guides. Don't feel as if you have to fill every space on the transparency—there may not be that many responses. Also, if you need more room on a graphic or if you would like to extend the lesson, feel free to add shapes.

▸ There will be many times when you're tempted to write outside the lines. Do! You don't want to give students the idea that a response must be only as long as the space provided.

▸ If you don't have time to complete an activity in one mini-lesson, allow students to fill in information as they discover it later. You may want to begin an activity and intentionally leave spaces for students to complete independently after the lesson.

▸ In some cases, you may want to show students the transparency before doing the reading or writing activity, to set a purpose and focus their attention.

▸ Stop and discuss ideas as you add them to the graphic organizers.

▸ Adapt the graphic organizers and mini-lessons as you see fit. Undoubtedly, you'll find wonderful ways to change or extend each lesson.

Assessment

Graphic organizers allow you to assess a student's comprehension at a glance. You can use the graphic organizers in this book to determine the depth of a student's understanding and the connections he or she has made. For example, you could have students read a nonfiction piece about a historical event and then complete the Cause-and-Effect Crab (page 51) to assess their comprehension of the multiple effects a single event can have.

Students can also use graphic organizers to assess their own learning. For example, after writing a persuasive essay or paragraph, have students complete the Persuasive Writing Fan (page 31) based on their piece. By filling in each section, they can assess whether they have included the basic structure of a persuasive essay or paragraph: introduction, three supporting points, and a conclusion. Students could also use the Word Trophies organizer (page 35) to write about three interesting words they included in their pieces.

Graphic organizers are a performance-based model of assessment and are ideal for including in student portfolios since they require students to demonstrate both their grasp of the concept and their reasoning.

Skills Matrix

	Reading								Writing									
	Pre-Reading	During Reading	After Reading	Making Connections	Comparing/Contrasting	Predicting	Making Inferences	Questioning	Traits: Ideas	Traits: Organization	Traits: Voice	Traits: Word Choice	Traits: Sentence Fluency	Traits: Conventions	Prewriting	Writing	Revising	Word Study
Character Traits in Action		●	●	●		●											●	
Comparing Settings		●	●	●	●						●							
Building Connections		●	●	●														
Truck On With Questions		●	●			●	●	●									●	
Comparison Tracks	●	●	●		●													
Idea Dragonfly									●						●			
Idea Lane									●						●			
Great Leads		●	●						●	●						●	●	
Persuasive Writing Fan									●	●					●	●	●	
Rhythm and Flow		●	●									●	●			●	●	
Word Trophies		●	●									●				●	●	●
Multiple Meanings		●	●									●				●	●	●
Balance a Word		●	●									●				●	●	
Word Ladder												●						●
Connect the Pieces		●	●	●			●								●			●
R.A.F.T		●	●						●		●				●	●	●	
Five W's Star		●	●						●	●					●	●	●	
ABC Chart	●	●	●	●					●			●			●			●
Cause-and-Effect Crab		●	●						●						●			
Flowchart		●	●						●	●					●			
Computer Grid		●	●		●												●	
Pinwheel Organizer		●	●						●	●					●	●	●	
Roller Coaster Story Map		●	●						●	●					●	●	●	
Setting Details		●	●						●		●	●			●	●	●	
Strategy Sun	●	●	●	●	●	●	●	●	●	●	●	●	●	●	●	●	●	●

Connections to the Standards

This book is designed to support you in meeting the following reading and writing standards outlined by Mid-continent Research for Education and Learning (McREL), an organization that collects and synthesizes national and state standards.

Reading
Uses the general skills and strategies of the reading process.

- Previews text (e.g., skims materials, uses pictures, textual clues, and text format).

- Establishes a purpose for reading (e.g., for information, for pleasure, to understand a specific viewpoint).

- Understands level-appropriate reading vocabulary (e.g., synonyms, antonyms, homophones, multimeaning words).

- Monitors own reading strategies and makes modifications as needed (e.g., recognizes when he or she is confused by a section of text, questions whether the text makes sense).

Uses reading skills and strategies to understand and interpret a variety of literary texts.

- Uses reading skills and strategies to understand a variety of literary passages and texts (e.g., fairy tales, folktales, fiction, nonfiction, myths, poems, fables, fantasies, historical fiction, biographies, autobiographies, chapter books).

- Understands the basic concept of plot (e.g., main problem, conflict, resolution, cause and effect).

- Understands similarities and differences within and among literary works from various genres and cultures (e.g., in terms of settings, character types, events, points of view, role of natural phenomena).

- Understands elements of character development in literary works (e.g., differences between main and minor characters; stereotypical characters as opposed to fully developed characters; changes that characters undergo; the importance of a character's actions, motives, and appearance to plot and theme).

- Makes connections between characters in simple events in a literary work and people and events in his or her own life.

Uses reading skills and strategies to understand and interpret a variety of informational texts.

- Summarizes and paraphrases information in texts (e.g., includes the main idea and significant supporting details of a reading selection).

- Uses prior knowledge and experience to understand and respond to new information.

- Understands structural patterns or organization in informational texts (e.g., chronological, logical, or sequential order; compare and contrast; cause and effect; proposition and support.)

Writing
Uses the general skills and strategies of the writing process.

- Prewriting: Uses prewriting strategies to plan written work (e.g., uses graphic organizers, story maps, and webs; groups related ideas; takes notes; brainstorms ideas;

organizes information according to type and purpose of writing.)

- Evaluates own and other's writing (e.g., determines the best features of a piece of writing, determines how own writing achieves its purposes, asks for feedback, responds to classmates' writing).

- Uses strategies (e.g., adapts focus, organization, point of view; determines knowledge and interests of audience) to write for different audiences (e.g., self, peers, teachers, adults).

- Uses strategies (e.g., adapts focus, point of view, organization, form) to write for a variety of purposes (e.g., to inform, entertain, explain, describe, record ideas).

- Writes expository compositions (e.g., identifies and stays on the topic; develops the topic with simple facts, details, examples, and explanations; excludes extraneous and inappropriate information; uses structures such as cause and effect, chronology, similarities and differences; uses several sources of information; provides concluding statement).

- Writes narrative accounts such as poems and stories (e.g., establishes a context that enables the reader to imagine the event or experience; develops characters, setting, plot; creates an organizing structure; sequences events; uses concrete sensory details, uses strategies such as dialogue, tension, and suspense; uses an identifiable voice).

- Writes autobiographical compositions (e.g., provides a context within which the incident occurs, uses simple narrative strategies, and provides some insight into why this incident is memorable).

- Writes expressive compositions (e.g., expresses ideas, reflections, and observations; uses an individual, authentic voice; uses narrative strategies, relevant details, and ideas that enable the reader to imagine the world of the event or experience).

- Writes in response to literature (e.g., summarizes main ideas and significant details; relates own ideas to supporting details; advances judgments; supports judgments with references to the text, other works, other authors, nonprint media, and personal knowledge).

Gathers and uses information for research purposes.

- Uses a variety of strategies to plan research (e.g., identifies possible topic by brainstorming, listing questions, using idea webs; organizes prior knowledge about a topic; develops a course of action; determines how to locate necessary information.)

- Uses strategies to compile information into written reports or summaries (e.g., incorporates notes into finished product; includes simple facts, details, explanations, and examples; draws conclusions from relationships and patterns that emerge from data from different sources; uses appropriate visual aids and media.)

Kendall, J. S., & Marzano, R. J. (2004). *Content knowledge: A compendium of standards and benchmarks for K–12 education.* Aurora, CO: Mid-continent Research for Education and Learning.

Online database:
http://www.mcrel.org/standards-benchmarks

References and Additional Resources

Baxendell, B. W. (2003). "Consistent, coherent, creative: The 3 C's of graphic organizers." *Teaching Exceptional Children, 35* (3), 46–53.

Bowman, L. A., Carpenter, J., & Paone, R. (1998). "Using graphic organizers, cooperative learning groups, and higher order thinking skills to improve reading comprehension." M.A. Action Research Project, Saint Xavier University.

Boyle, J. R. & Weishaar, M. (1997)."The effects of expert-generated versus student-generated cognitive organizers on the reading comprehension of students with learning disabilities." *Learning Disabilities Research and Practice, 12* (4), 228–235.

Bromley, K., Irwin-De Vitis, L., & Modlo, M. (1995). *Graphic organizers: Visual strategies for active learning.* New York: Scholastic.

Chang, K. E., Sung, Y. T., & Chen, I. D. (2002). "The effects of concept mapping to enhance text comprehension and summarization." *Journal of Experimental Education, 71* (1), 5–24.

Dodge, J. (2005). *Differentiation in action.* New York: Scholastic.

Egan, M. (1999). "Reflections on effective use of graphic organizers." *Journal of Adolescent and Adult Literacy, 42* (8), 641.

Ellis, E. S. (1994). "Integrating writing strategy instruction with content-area instruction: Part I—Orienting students to organizational devices." *Intervention in School and Clinic, 29* (3), 169.

Ellis, E. S. (1994). "Integrating writing instruction with content area instruction: Part II—Writing processes." *Intervention in School and Clinic, 29* (4), 219–230.

Gil-Garcia, A. & Villegas, J. (2003). "Engaging minds, enhancing comprehension and constructing knowledge through visual representations." Paper presented at a conference on word association for case method research and application: Bordeaux, France.

Guastello, E. F. (2000). "Concept mapping effects on science-content comprehension of low-achieving inner-city seventh graders." *Remedial and Special Education*, *21* (6), 356.

Hyerle, D. (1995–1996). *"Thinking maps: Seeing is understanding."* *Educational Leadership*, *53* (4), 85–89.

Jacobson, J. (1999). *The big book of graphic organizers*. New York: Scholastic.

Kim, A-H, Vaughn, S., Wanzek, J., & Wei, S. (2004). "Graphic organizers and their effects on the reading comprehension of students with learning disabilities: A synthesis of research." *Journal of Learning Disabilities*, *37* (2), 105–118.

Merkley, D. M., & Jeffries, D. (2001). "Guidelines for implementing a graphic organizer." *Reading Teacher*, *54* (4), 350.

Moore, D. & Readence, J. (1984). "A quantitative and qualitative review of graphic organizer research." *Journal of Educational Research*, *78* (1), 11–17.

Robb, Anina. (2003). *40 Graphic organizers that build comprehension during independent reading*. New York: Scholastic.

Shanahan, T. (2005). *The national reading panel report: Practical advice for teachers.* Chicago: Learning Point Associates (NCREL).

Van Zile, S. (2006). *Reading and writing: Graphic organizers and mini-lessons.* New York: Scholastic.

Westwater, A. & Wolfe, P. (2000). "The brain compatible curriculum." *Educational Leadership*.

- Identifying Character Traits

- Making Inferences

Character Traits in Action

Purpose

In this activity, students discern a character's traits by observing his or her actions, thoughts, feelings, and beliefs. This helps students focus on how skillful writers reveal character traits in subtle ways—an understanding that will improve students' reading comprehension and can be applied to their own writing.

Introducing the Activity

Point out to students that authors rarely tell us what characters are like; instead, they demonstrate characters' traits through showing us their behavior, choices, thoughts, feelings, and beliefs.

Using the Overhead Transparency

1. In preparation for the lesson, select a text in which a character's traits are revealed—for example, one in which a character takes action, expresses an opinion, reacts to an experience, makes a choice, or thinks through a problem.

2. Read the passage aloud to students, and then display the overhead transparency.

3. Choose a quotation or descriptive excerpt from the passage you read and record it in one of the "Evidence From Book" boxes; add the page number on which it appears in the book. Then ask, "What does this action tell you about the character? What trait have you observed?" Encourage thoughtful, specific responses and record them beside the label "Trait" on the overhead.

4. Choose two additional passages from the same text that show two different traits for the same character. Read the passages aloud and complete the rest of the graphic organizer as described above.

5. Provide photocopies of the reproducible for students to use as reading response for other texts.

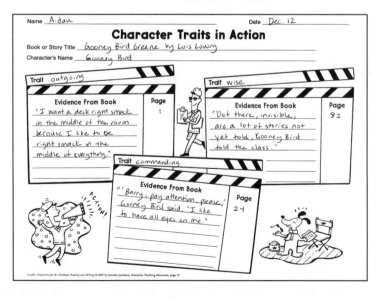

Name Aidan   Date Dec. 12

Character Traits in Action

Book or Story Title Gooney Bird Greene by Lois Lowry
Character's Name Gooney Bird

Trait outgoing

Evidence From Book   Page
"I want a desk right smack   1
in the middle of the room
because I like to be
right smack in the
middle of everything."

Trait wise

Evidence From Book   Page
"Out there, invisible,   82
are a lot of stories not
yet told," Gooney Bird
told the class."

Trait commanding

Evidence From Book   Page
"Barry, pay attention, please,"   24
Gooney Bird said. "I like
to have all eyes on me."

Graphic Organizers for the Overhead: Reading and Writing © 2007 by Jennifer Jacobson, Scholastic Teaching Resources, page 13

Taking It Further

▶ Have students complete the graphic organizer by filling in the traits of a celebrity or historical figure. Encourage students to avoid words that don't have much impact on the reader (such as *nice* or *fun*)—and to choose instead more descriptive, precise words.

▶ Ask members of a reading group to select different characters from the same book and complete the graphic organizer about them. Allow time for everyone in the group to share his or her discoveries and compare characters.

Name _____

Date _____

Character Traits in Action

Book or Story Title _____

Character's Name _____

Trait

Evidence From Book

Page

Trait

Evidence From Book

Page

Trait

Evidence From Book

Page

Trait

Evidence From Book

Page

ACTION!

Reading

• Understanding
Setting

• Making
Text-to-Self and
Text-to-Text
Connections

Comparing Settings

Purpose

By comparing one setting with another, students develop an understanding of the importance of setting to a reader's experience. This graphic organizer also supports reading comprehension by providing a format for text-to-self and text-to-text comparisons.

Introducing the Activity

Explain to students that the details of a setting include time, place, and atmosphere, and can be drawn from the text or illustrations, or inferred from what the narrator or characters say. Briefly engage students in a discussion of your classroom setting. Encourage them to note the physical environment, the surrounding landscape, the mood of the day, and the point in time.

Using the Overhead Transparency

1. In preparation for the lesson, choose two settings to compare. Consider comparing any of the following: two settings within one story, the setting of a book and the setting in which your students live, or the same setting in two different time periods.

2. Display the overhead transparency. With students' guidance, make a brief sketch representing one of the settings in the oval on the left.

3. Ask students to describe the setting in detail, and record key words at the bottom of the page. Then repeat the process with the second setting. Finally, ask students to decide what the settings have in common, and record this information under the heading "Both."

4. Distribute copies of the reproducible to students, and provide them with a new focus for comparison, using either the same or another text.

Taking It Further

▶ Use this graphic organizer to compare retellings of favorite folktales in which the settings differ. Discuss how changing one literary element, such as the setting, helps to create an entirely new story.

▶ Many stories include a change of setting that offers wonderful opportunities for comparison. For example, in *Yolanda's Genius*, by Carol Fenner (Margaret K. McElderry, 1995), Yolanda moves from the bustle of Chicago to the quiet life of Grand River, Michigan. After reading this story, have students compare the urban and rural settings.

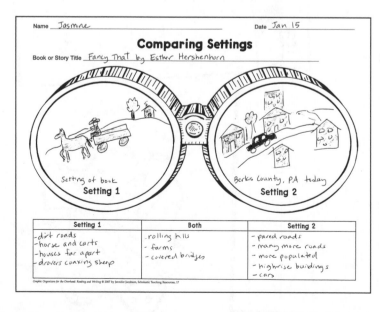

Name _____ Date _____

Comparing Settings

Book or Story Title _____

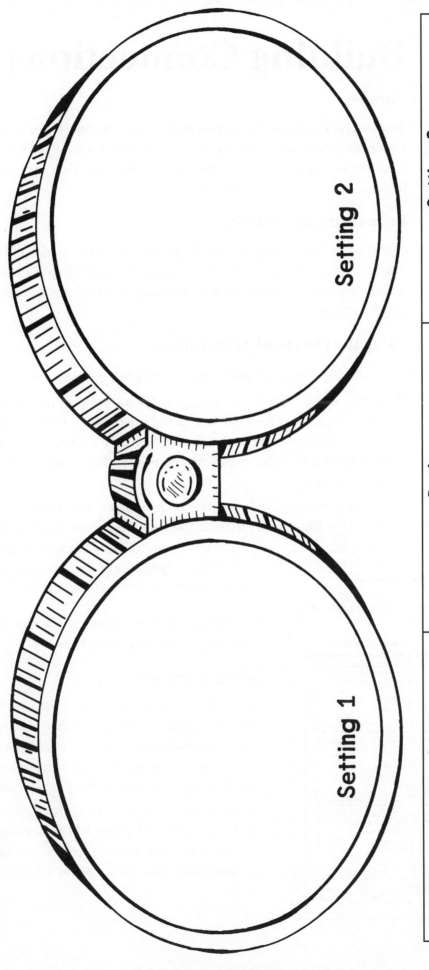

Setting 2

Setting 1

Setting 1	Both	Setting 2

Building Connections

Purpose

This graphic organizer encourages students to pay close attention to personal responses to text and record the connections they make. When readers connect literature to their own experiences, they increase both their comprehension of the text and their level of engagement with it.

Introducing the Activity

Tell students that because readers bring their own experiences and knowledge to what they read, every reader's experience is unique. Explain that today's graphic organizer will help them understand how each reader relates to a text in a different way.

Using the Overhead Transparency

1. Read aloud a poem or an excerpt from a piece of literature.

2. Display the overhead transparency. In the top window under "What I Read," record a quotation from the text. Distribute copies of the graphic organizer and ask students to write the quotation on their copies. Then ask questions, such as "What memories did this piece of writing conjure for you? Did it inspire any questions?"

3. Record your response in the top window under "It Reminds Me Of." Give students a few minutes to write their own responses. Allow a few students to share what they wrote. Share your response as well, and affirm the importance of diverse, unique connections to text. Complete the rest of the page in the same way.

4. Distribute additional copies of the reproducible for students to use with other texts.

Taking It Further

▶ To emphasize the uniqueness of individual responses to literature, have students share their connections during a literature group. Create a large chart paper version of the graphic organizer. Each group member can record his or her thoughts on a lined sticky note and post it on the chart.

▶ To allow for uninterrupted reading, have students use sticky notes to mark places where they have made connections. Later they can go back, reread the marked passages, and record them on the graphic organizer.

Name _____   Date _____

Building Connections

Book or Story Title _____

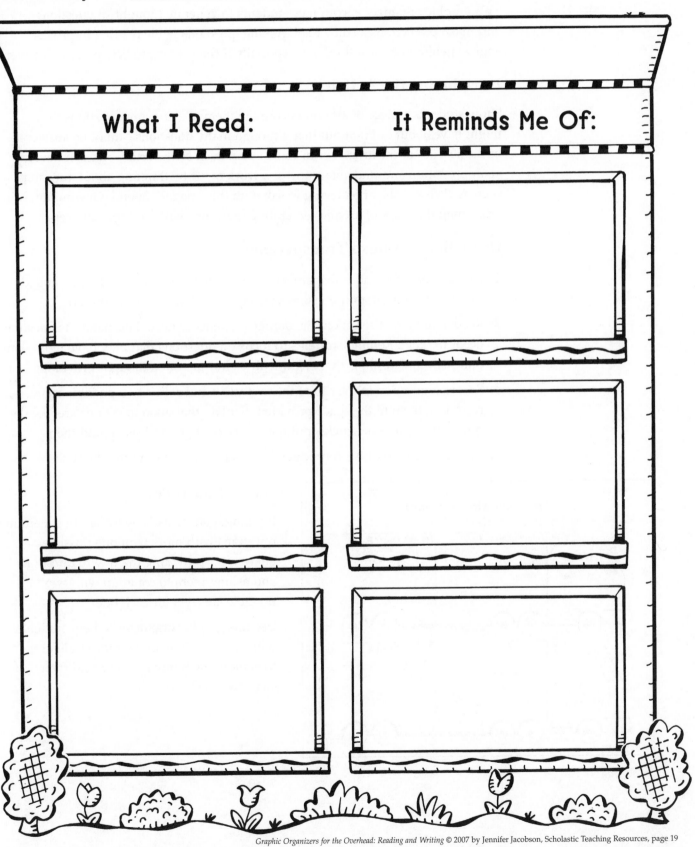

What I Read: **It Reminds Me Of:**

Graphic Organizers for the Overhead: Reading and Writing © 2007 by Jennifer Jacobson, Scholastic Teaching Resources, page 19

Truck On With Questions

Purpose

This graphic organizer encourages students to generate thoughtful questions and make predictions as they read. Asking questions while reading improves engagement and critical thinking, especially if the reader predicts possible answers.

Introducing the Activity

Show students a piece of art and encourage them to share any questions they might have about it. Point out that although many questions cannot be answered in the absence of the artist—or in some cases, even *by* the artist—we can develop an appreciation and understanding of a work of art by thinking about questions such as "What is the artist trying to say with this image?" Spend a few minutes examining the work of art and generating questions with multiple answers.

Using the Overhead Transparency

1. Display the overhead transparency. Explain that readers can ask open-ended questions about literature just as viewers can ask questions about art.

2. Read aloud a text selection. Encourage students to raise their hands as questions occur to them. Remind students to focus on questions that may have more than one answer. Questions that begin with "why" are often thought provoking.

3. Record a question in the cab of the first truck and solicit two possible answers, recording them in the space provided. Explain that good questions are like the powerful engines on trucks, pulling a variety of good ideas behind them.

4. Distribute copies of the reproducible for students to use with other texts.

Taking It Further

▶ If younger students have difficulty generating questions with more than one possible answer, try providing them with questions and asking them to come up with two possible answers for each one.

▶ Use this graphic organizer to help students with story writing. Encourage students to explore the motivations behind their characters' actions.

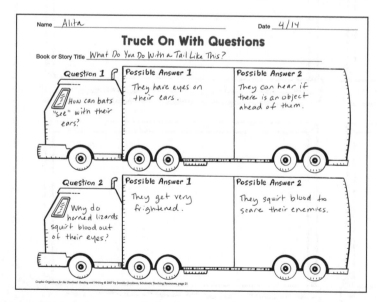

Truck On With Questions

Book or Story Title _____

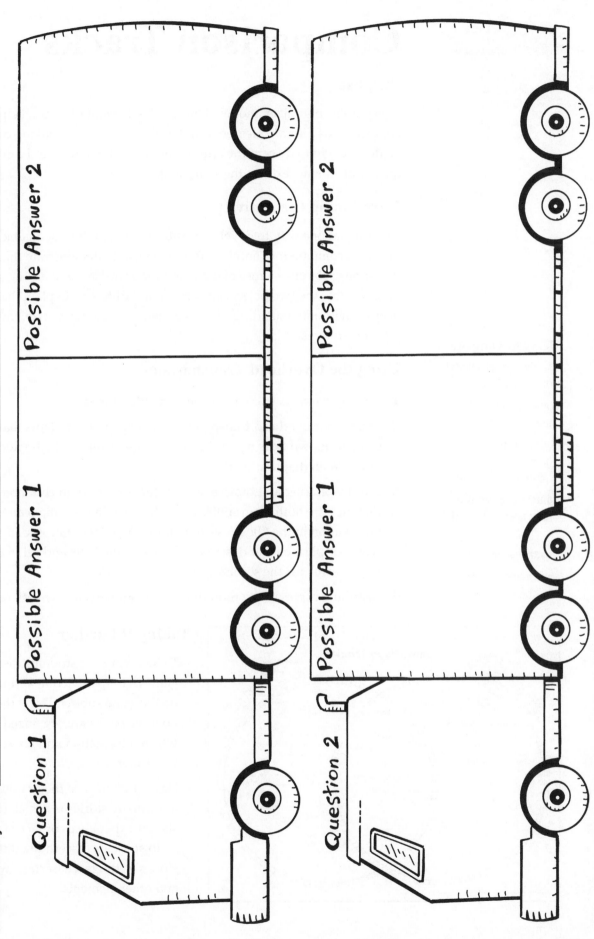

Question 1

Possible Answer 1

Possible Answer 2

Question 2

Possible Answer 1

Possible Answer 2

Reading

• Comparing
  Texts and
  Genres

• Analyzing
  Author's Style

Comparison Tracks

Purpose

This graphic organizer, modeled on the classic Venn diagram, helps students compare texts, literary elements, and authors' styles. By making comparisons, students begin to discern the criteria for particular genres and can evaluate the quality of similar texts on the same subject.

Introducing the Activity

Explain that one way to develop a better understanding of an object or even an idea is to compare it to another. You may wish to demonstrate this by displaying two similar objects—a rose and a daisy, for example—and asking students to describe how the two objects are similar and different. Explain that in order to deepen their understanding of a book, genre, or author's style, they will compare it to something similar.

Using the Overhead Transparency

1. Choose two texts to compare. See list at left for ideas.

2. Display the overhead transparency and explain to students that they will be comparing two texts using the graphic organizer. Write the titles and explain how a Venn diagram works.

3. Start by offering an example of what the texts have in common—for instance, that they are both biographies or are both set in the American South. Enter this information in the "Both" section of the organizer. Ask students to think of words or phrases that describe only one of the texts and fill in this information. Do the same for the second text.

4. Distribute copies of the reproducible for students to use with other texts.

Texts to Compare

* nonfiction selections on the same topic

* biographies about the same person

* books in the same genre (such as mysteries or fantasies)

* different versions of fairy tales or legends

* books or short stories by the same author

* newspaper articles on the same topic

Taking It Further

▶ To help younger students distinguish between genres, compare fiction and nonfiction texts on the same subject. Draw their attention to how the books are organized and the ways in which information and ideas are revealed to the reader.

▶ Have students use the graphic organizer to compare stories in which characters have similar experiences or face similar choices. Help students discern the differences in the stories' settings, characters, writing style, and other elements.

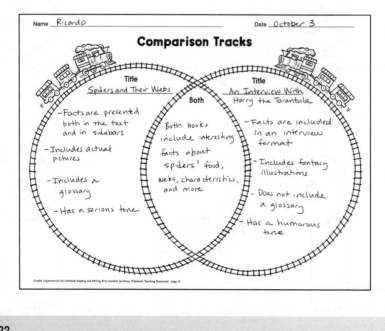

Name _____

Date _____

Comparison Tracks

Title

Both

Title

Idea Dragonfly

Purpose

This graphic organizer allows students to focus on and personalize a writing topic in order to create a more meaningful essay or story.

Introducing the Activity

Ask students to imagine they are reporters for a local newspaper assigned to write an article about their school. Guide them to an understanding that "school" is too broad a subject to be covered in an article. Explain that today's graphic organizer offers a way to make a broad idea more focused and interesting.

Using the Overhead Transparency

1. Display the overhead transparency and write "School" in the flower.

2. Divide the class into small groups or pairs and ask them to brainstorm specific, more focused ideas that connect to the topic. Then share ideas as a class, discussing which ones would make interesting and manageable articles and why.

3. Choose four strong, specific ideas to write in the dragonfly's wings. As you record them, note the variety of ways in which students narrowed and personalized the topic—for instance, by noting a timely issue or by focusing on a personal experience.

4. Distribute copies of the reproducible. Either provide students with a new topic or ask them to select a topic from a list of options. Ask students to work individually to generate four specific, focused ideas for writing about the topic.

Taking It Further

▶ Try the activity in reverse! Read an interesting personal essay. Write the author's main idea on one of the wings. Ask students to figure out what broader topic may have inspired the writer's more specific idea and write it in the flower. Have students brainstorm other ideas the author could have chosen about this topic.

▶ Ask students to think of a writing topic and write it in the flower. Then collect the organizers and place them in your writing center. Suggest that students looking for a writing idea choose one of the writing topics and narrow it further.

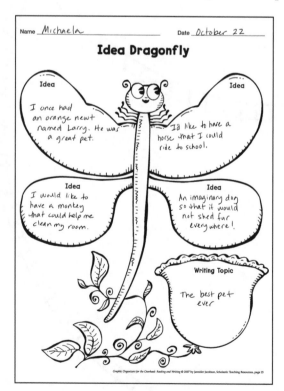

Name _Michaela_   Date _October 22_

Idea Dragonfly

Idea
I once had an orange newt named Larry. He was a great pet.

Idea
I'd like to have a horse that I could ride to school.

Idea
I would like to have a monkey that could help me clean my room.

Idea
An imaginary dog so that it would not shed fur everywhere!

Writing Topic
The best pet ever

Graphic Organizers for the Overhead: Reading and Writing © 2007 by Jennifer Jacobson, Scholastic Teaching Resources, page 25

Name _____ Date _____

Idea Dragonfly

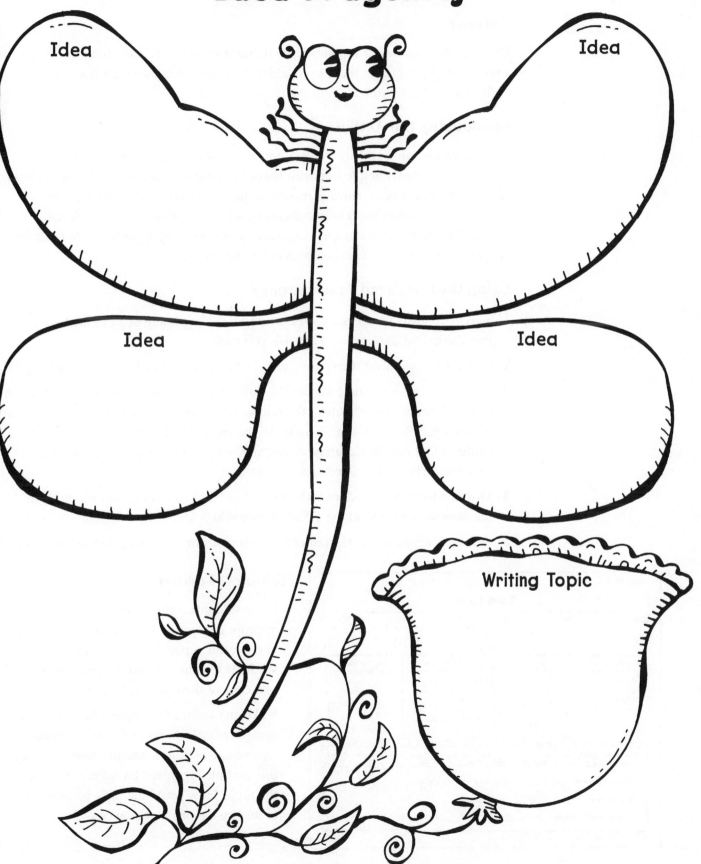

Idea

Idea

Idea

Idea

Writing Topic

Idea Lane

Purpose

This activity encourages students to be thoughtful and selective when choosing a writing topic. It guides them to consider their audience, the breadth and depth of their topic, the organization of the piece, and more.

Introducing the Activity

Discuss the idea that embarking on a new piece of writing is a big commitment; a writer has to be willing to live with his or her project through first drafts, revisions, editing, and publishing. For that reason, writers often consider—and try out— a number of different ideas before choosing which one they want to stick with. Tell students that today's graphic organizer gives them an opportunity to consider the pros and cons of an idea before deciding to "move in."

Using the Overhead Transparency

1. Select two ideas for an essay—for example, the beginning of an unlikely friendship and the story of a big risk you took.

2. Display the overhead transparency, and write one idea on the roof of each house.

3. Begin with one idea and consider its positive aspects aloud. Record these thoughts in note form on the left side of the house. Next, consider the possible drawbacks of this topic. Record these thoughts on the right side. Explain to students that drawbacks aren't necessarily a reason to drop an idea; in fact, they can be helpful in developing the idea.

4. Move on to your second idea, thinking aloud and recording your thoughts in the same way. Still thinking aloud, decide which idea seems stronger.

5. Distribute copies of the reproducible for students to use when selecting essay topics.

Taking It Further

▶ Have students write two ideas in the appropriate spaces on the graphic organizer and exchange pages with a partner. Allow students to consider and discuss the pros and cons of their partner's ideas.

▶ Make an overhead transparency of a personal essay that lacks focus or interest. (Do not choose one of your students' essays.) Using this graphic organizer, have students evaluate the topic. How could the topic be reworked to inspire a more engaging essay?

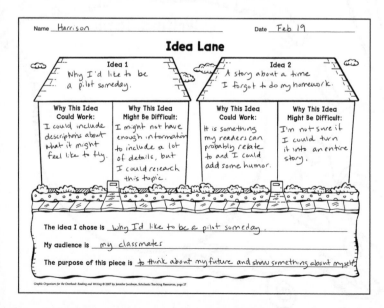

Name _____   Date _____

Idea Lane

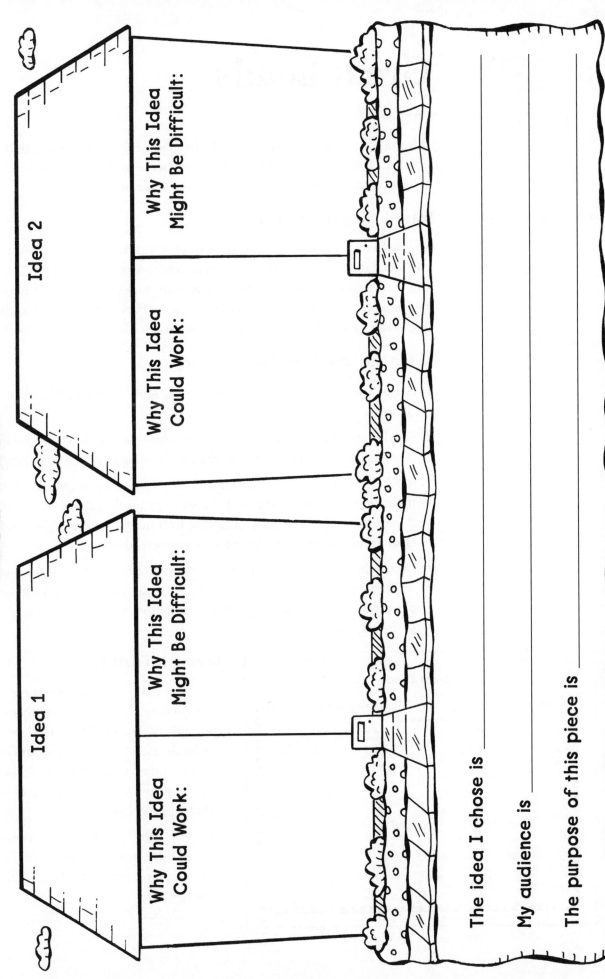

Idea 2

Why This Idea Could Work:

Why This Idea Might Be Difficult:

Idea 1

Why This Idea Could Work:

Why This Idea Might Be Difficult:

The idea I chose is _____

My audience is _____

The purpose of this piece is _____

Great Leads

Purpose

This graphic organizer encourages students to compare and evaluate the ways in which authors invite readers into a piece of writing. It can also be used to help writers create and revise leads for a variety of written pieces.

Strategies for Leads

* a question
* a description of a character or setting
* a sound (onomatopoeia)
* a bold fact or statement
* an anecdote
* dialogue

Introducing the Activity

Choose two examples of leads (not from students' writing). After reading each lead aloud, ask, "Do you feel inspired to continue reading? What is it about this lead that captures your interest—or fails to capture your interest?" Explain that the beginning of a story, article, or essay must "hook" the reader into the piece. Discuss and list different strategies writers use for leads (see list at left).

Using the Overhead Transparency

1. Gather a stack of grade-appropriate books and/or articles that feature a variety of leads.

2. Display the overhead transparency. Tell students that they will use this graphic organizer to examine the many ways authors begin pieces of writing.

3. Read aloud one lead and complete the top row of the graphic organizer, filling in the title of the piece, the lead, the strategy used, and whether it works. Repeat the exercise with a contrasting lead from a different piece. Add to the class list of strategies as you come across new ideas.

4. Divide the class into small groups. Give each group copies of the reproducible and three pieces of writing with different leads. Instruct groups to read one piece at a time and fill in the graphic organizer. Invite students to add strategies to the class list.

Taking It Further

▶ Invite small groups to share the leads of essays they've written. Have them use the graphic organizer to keep track of the types of leads used by group members and whether they were effective. Encourage students to use peer feedback to adjust their approaches.

▶ Have students write three different leads for a single piece of writing and then use the graphic organizer to help them select the best one.

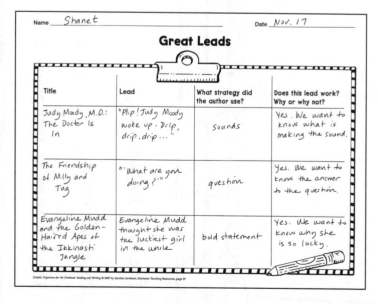

Name _Shanet_   Date _Nov. 17_

Great Leads

Title	Lead	What strategy did the author use?	Does this lead work? Why or why not?
Judy Moody, M.D.: The Doctor Is In	"Plip! Judy Moody woke up. Drip, drip, drip..."	sounds	Yes. We want to know what is making the sound.
The Friendship of Milly and Tug	"What are you doing?"	question	Yes. We want to know the answer to the question.
Evangeline Mudd and the Golden-Haired Apes of the Ikkinasti Jungle	Evangeline Mudd thought she was the luckiest girl in the whole	bold statement	Yes. We want to know why she is so lucky.

Graphic Organizers for the Overhead: Reading and Writing © 2007 by Jennifer Jacobson, Scholastic Teaching Resources, page 29

Name _____

Great Leads

Title	Lead	What strategy did the author use?	Does this lead work? Why or why not?

Persuasive Writing Fan

Purpose

This graphic organizer helps students organize ideas for a persuasive essay and identify examples of supporting evidence. The shape of the graphic organizer supports an understanding of the relationship between the essay's introduction, body, and conclusion.

Introducing the Activity

Explain that a persuasive essay has several key components: the introduction or the statement of purpose, three paragraphs of supportive arguments, and a concluding paragraph in which the argument is strongly restated. Share a sample persuasive essay and ask students to identify the components.

Using the Overhead Transparency

1. Display the overhead transparency and note its shape. Point out that the introduction states the writer's point of view and draws the reader into the piece, the three points support the main idea, and the conclusion brings the points together and restates the main idea.

2. Provide students with a controversial topic—for example, summer homework—and guide them in stating a point of view about it. Choose one point of view and write it in the Introduction section.

3. Help students come up with three strong arguments that support the point of view. Finally, compose a conclusion. Guide students to clearly restate the point of view. They might also direct readers to take action based on the evidence presented.

4. Distribute copies of the reproducible and invite students to plan a persuasive essay supporting the opposing side of the argument (or invite them to choose a different topic).

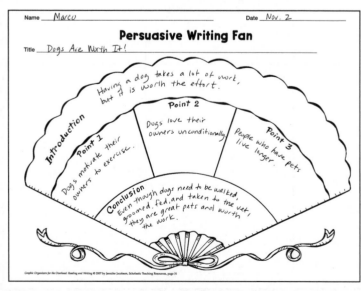

Taking It Further

Have students use the graphic organizer to plan a persuasive essay. Then have them share their completed essays in small groups while group members listen and fill in a graphic organizer with the information they hear. Do the maps match? Why or why not?

Name _____

Date _____

Persuasive Writing Fan

Title _____

Introduction

Point 1

Point 2

Point 3

Conclusion

Graphic Organizers for the Overhead: Reading and Writing © 2007 by Jennifer Jacobson, Scholastic Teaching Resources, page 31

Rhythm and Flow

Purpose

This graphic organizer helps students understand how authors craft strong sentences and paragraphs. In examining both the structure of individual sentences and the variety of sentences within paragraphs, students become more sensitive to the role of rhythm in their writing.

Introducing the Activity

Tell students that they will be using a graphic organizer to help them search for sentences they like and figure out what makes them well written. Explain that they will need to consider not just how a sentence sounds on its own but what role the sentence plays in the paragraph.

Using the Overhead Transparency

1. Choose a short paragraph that includes a variety of sentence structures and read it aloud.

2. In the first column of the graphic organizer, write each sentence of the paragraph separately (as a list). Write the first two words of each sentence in the second column. Cover all but the first sentence and ask a volunteer to read it aloud.

3. Ask students to describe the sound and feeling of the sentence using specific adjectives, such as *musical*, *lively*, *sharp*, or *smooth*. Record student descriptions in the third column. Draw a horizontal line below these first entries. Continue to fill in the rest of the page in the same way.

4. Look at the second column. Discuss how the beginning of each sentence affects the overall feeling of the sentence. Guide students to an understanding that varying sentence beginnings and lengths within a paragraph helps create rhythm and flow.

5. Distribute copies of the reproducible for students to use with other texts or to analyze their own writing.

Taking It Further

Provide students with a long sentence. Have them rewrite the sentence in four different ways. Use the graphic organizer to compare the rhythm and flow of each sentence.

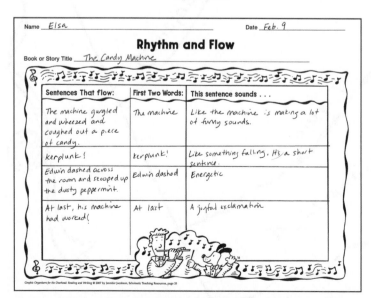

Name _Elsa_   Date _Feb. 9_

Rhythm and Flow

Book or Story Title _The Candy Machine_

Sentences That flow:	First Two Words:	This sentence sounds . . .
The machine gurgled and wheezed and coughed out a piece of candy.	The machine	Like the machine is making a lot of funny sounds.
kerplunk!	kerplunk!	Like something falling. It's a short sentence.
Edwin dashed across the room and scooped up the dusty peppermint.	Edwin dashed	Energetic
At last, his machine had worked!	At last	A joyful exclamation

Name _____

Date _____

Rhythm and Flow

Book or Story Title _____

Sentences That Flow:	First Two Words:	This sentence sounds . . . .

Word Trophies

Purpose

This graphic organizer helps students note examples of exemplary word choice in texts. It can also be used for self-assessment in writing or to assist students in providing peer support in writing conferences.

Introducing the Activity

Instruct students to write what comes to mind when they hear the word *vehicle*. Ask several volunteers to share what they recorded. Point out that because you used a vague term, each student pictured it differently. Had you said "mud-splattered green Jeep" or "sleek black limousine," you could have communicated a clearer image. Explain that this graphic organizer helps students notice effective word choice as well as find and use just the right words in their own writing.

Using the Overhead Transparency

1. Read aloud a poem or brief excerpt from a longer text. When you are finished, ask students whether any of the words you read stuck with them. Ask a volunteer to share a memorable word.

2. Display the overhead transparency and record the word in the top part of a trophy. Then ask, "What is it about the word that made it memorable?" After hearing from several different students, paraphrase their responses on the base of the trophy.

3. Fill in the other two trophies in the same way with other memorable words from the piece. Help students identify why the words are effective: for instance, because they are precise, figurative, alliterative, or rhythmic, or because they help create vivid images or appeal to the senses.

4. Distribute copies of the reproducible for students to use with other texts.

Taking It Further

Suggest that students read their own writing to find places where they could be more specific—for example, did they write "candy" when they could have written "lemon drops"? Have them record the new words on the graphic organizer and include their reasoning for using these words.

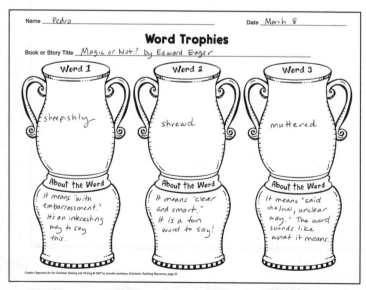

Name _____

Date _____

Word Trophies

Book or Story Title _____

Word 1

About the Word

Word 2

About the Word

Word 3

About the Word

• Understanding
  Parts of Speech

• Recognizing
  Multiple
  Meanings

Multiple Meanings

Purpose

This activity engages students while building vocabulary, supporting reading comprehension, and helping students select strong and accurate words in their writing.

Introducing the Activity

Offer students a word that has many different meanings. Ask students to consider the different meanings and also how the meanings may be related. For instance, the verb *to bug* means "to annoy." Perhaps that's because bugs can be annoying! A *bug* is also a tiny listening device. Is it called a bug because it is the size of a bug?

Using the Overhead Transparency

1. Display the overhead transparency. In the box at the bottom of the page, write a word that has many meanings, such as *case*. Ask, "Who can think of a meaning for this word?"

2. Ask a volunteer to provide a meaning and think of a person who might use the word with that meaning. Then ask the volunteer to use the word in a sentence that this person might say. For example, "A teenager might use the word in a sentence like 'Get off my case!'" Record the speaker (in this case "teenager") in one of the figures and the sample sentence in the appropriate speech balloon.

3. Ask another volunteer to think of an alternate meaning, name a possible speaker, and offer a sample sentence. Record the new entries.

4. Have students work individually or in pairs to come up with at least three additional speakers and meanings for the word. Invite students to share their work with the class.

5. Distribute copies of the reproducible. Have students use it to record words with multiple meanings that they encounter in their reading.

Taking It Further

As you record sentences in the speech balloons, have students provide the word's part of speech. For example: "There is milk in the dairy *case*." (noun) "The criminal *cased* the joint." (verb)

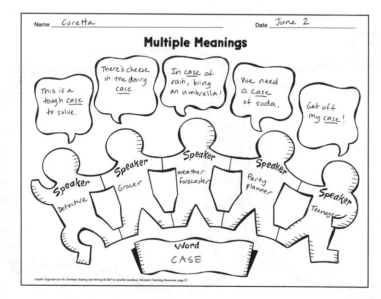

Multiple Meanings

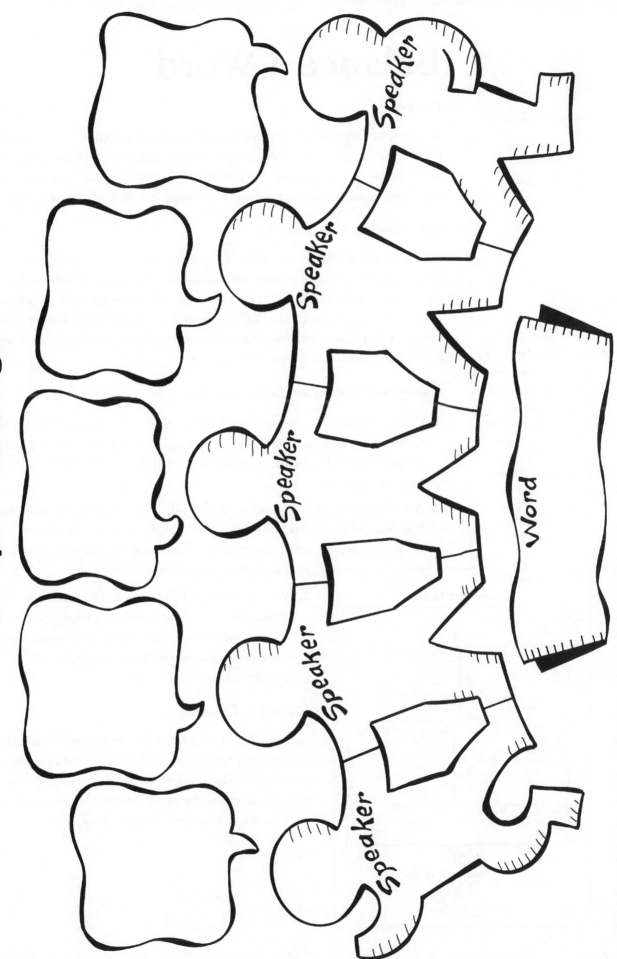

Vocabulary
and
Word Choice

• Building
  Vocabulary
• Word Choice

Balance a Word

Purpose

This graphic organizer helps students use background knowledge—their own and their classmates'—to build vocabulary. Discussions such as those inspired by this activity, in which knowledge is "pooled" and selected words are used repeatedly, encourage students to incorporate new words into their speech and writing.

Introducing the Activity

Discuss the idea that we are aware of more words than we actually use in conversation. However, even if we're familiar with certain words because we've read them in a book or article or have heard others use them, we might have trouble defining these words. Tell students that during the following activity, they will pool their knowledge as a class in order to develop a clear understanding of a word they don't yet use in conversation.

Using the Overhead Transparency

1. Choose a word that students are likely to have heard or read but do not use in their own speech or writing. (Do not choose a word that is totally unfamiliar.) Display the overhead transparency and write the word at the top of the graphic organizer.

2. Ask, "What do you know about this word? You might tell me what you think it means, when it might or might not be used, or what part of speech it is. Or you might use it in a sentence or tell me an antonym or synonym." Fill in the information on the page in any order.

3. Provide small groups with copies of the reproducible and an assortment of new words to investigate. You might select words from a read-aloud or curriculum-related text in order to increase students' comprehension and retention of information.

Taking It Further

Each week, have students choose a word from their independent reading and fill in the graphic organizer for that word. Invite students to discuss the words together in order to complete the page. Compile the words in alphabetical order to create a handy reference book.

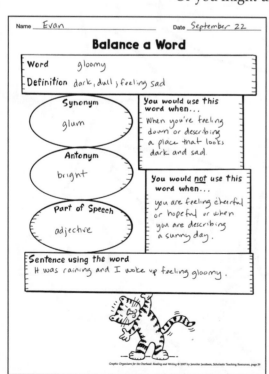

Balance a Word

Word

Definition

Synonym

Antonym

Part of Speech

You would use this word when...

You would <u>not</u> use this word when...

Sentence using the word

Vocabulary
and
Word Choice

Recognizing
Word
Relationships

Word Ladder

Purpose

This graphic organizer makes a game of exploring word structures and word families. It helps students discover patterns and improve spelling skills. Older students can practice using prefixes and suffixes.

Introducing the Activity

Explain that many words are related to one another, like members of an enormous extended family. Tell students that they will play a game that involves discovering unexpected ways in which some words are related to others.

Using the Overhead Transparency

1. Display the overhead transparency. Tell students that the object of the game is to construct a ladder of words. Each new word on the ladder must be related to the last, according to a particular rule. See list at left for ideas.

2. Begin the first round by writing a compound word in the space at the bottom of the ladder. Tell students that in order to move up the ladder, they must change one of the two words to make a new compound word. Here's an example of a way to complete the ladder, from the bottom up:

overhaul—overcoat—raincoat—rainbow—bowlegged

Point out that *overhaul* and *bowlegged* don't appear to be related, but the words that come between connect them.

3. Provide student pairs with copies of the graphic organizer. Tell them a new rule for the game and give them a beginning word. Have the pairs work together to climb to the top rung.

Taking It Further

Keep plenty of copies of this graphic organizer on hand, along with a deck of index cards containing rules for additional challenges. This makes a great five-minute challenge when you have a few minutes of extra time before lunch, at the end of the day, or in between activities.

Possible "Rules" to Move Up the Ladder:

* Change one letter in a word to make a new word (*score, scare, stare, start, smart*)
* Provide rhyming words (*stumbling, mumbling, fumbling, crumbling, tumbling*)
* Provide synonyms (*carry, transport, bring, cart, tote*)
* Change the prefix or suffix to make a new word (*focus, refocus, refocused, focused, focusing*)

Name Corinne   Date January 18

Word Ladder

horseback

horseshoe

snowshoe

snowball

baseball

Graphic Organizers for the Overhead: Reading and Writing © 2007 by Jennifer Jacobson, Scholastic Teaching Resources, page 41

Word Ladder

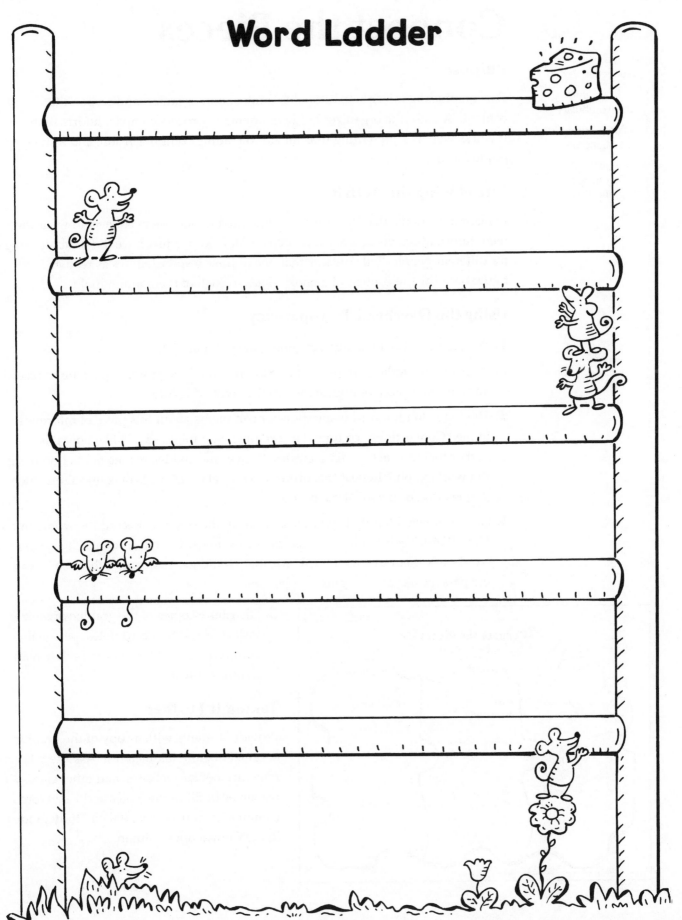

Flexible Use

• Comprehending Nonfiction Text

• Integrating New Vocabulary

• Summarizing Key Concepts

• Making Text-to-Self Connections

Connect the Pieces

Purpose

This graphic organizer helps students think about, organize, and respond to content. Because the organizer guides students to process complex information, it works well as a prewriting tool, an aid to reading comprehension, and a study guide for tests.

Introducing the Activity

Explain to students that this activity is intended to help them connect to what they read. Information, vocabulary, and ideas contained in a text have different meanings for different people. Tell students that one of their responsibilities as readers is to figure out how the content of a book relates to each of them individually.

Using the Overhead Transparency

1. Read aloud a brief passage containing factual material.

2. Display the overhead transparency. Slowly reread the passage, pausing to record an important piece of information in the "Notes" column.

3. Thinking aloud, record inspirations or comments about this piece of information in the "Connections" column. For example, you might say, "I like how this author included actual diary entries. It gives me an idea for the nonfiction piece I'm working on." Repeat this process to model other types of connections, such as questions or personal memories.

4. Have students identify key vocabulary from the passage. Record the words in the "Key Words" column and discuss their meanings. To help students choose key words, ask them to search for words that would give someone who hasn't read the passage a chance of guessing its topic.

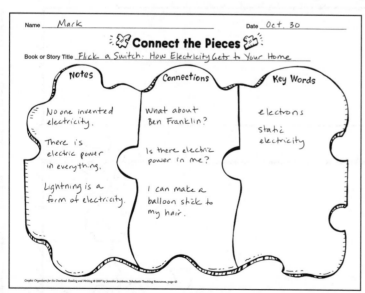

5. Distribute copies of the graphic organizer. Ask students to record notes, personal connections, and key words as they read a different text.

Taking It Further

Provide students with a copy of the graphic organizer before taking a test. Ask them to use reference books, websites, and other classroom resources to fill in the Notes and Key Words columns, then personalize their study guides in the Connections column.

Name _____

Date _____

✂️ Connect the Pieces 🧩

Book or Story Title _____

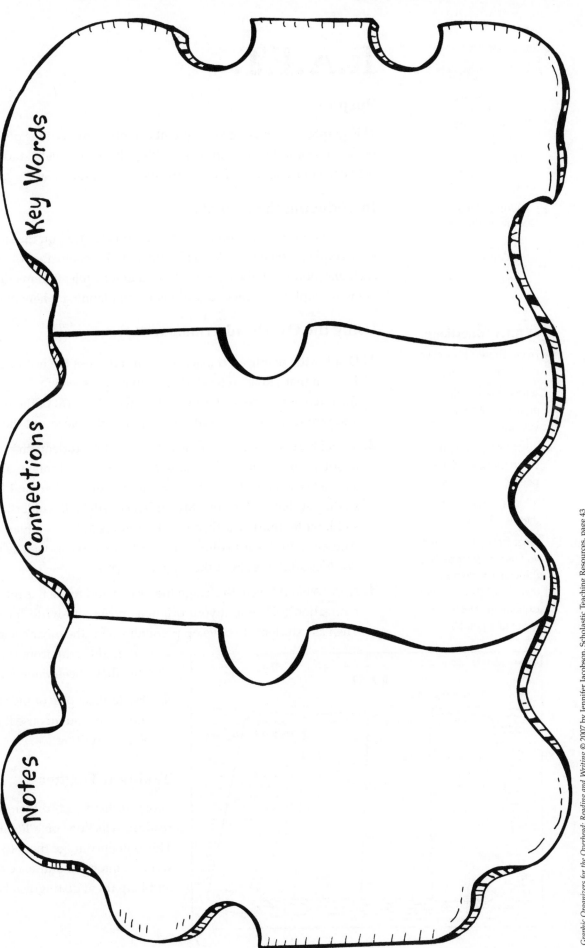

Key Words

Connections

Notes

Graphic Organizers for the Overhead: Reading and Writing © 2007 by Jennifer Jacobson, Scholastic Teaching Resources, page 43

R.A.F.T. Questions

- From whose perspective is this piece written?

- Who is the intended audience? How can you tell?

- What format does the writing follow? Is it a poem? Story? Essay?

- What is the topic of the piece?

- What strong verb could you use to describe what the writer is doing in this piece? (Is the writer explaining? Describing? Arguing a point?)

R.A.F.T.

Purpose

This graphic organizer gives students an opportunity to experiment with perspective and purpose in their writing. It can also help students distinguish between genres and think critically about what they read.

Introducing the Activity

Choose a pair of brief, contrasting selections focused on the same topic, such as a biographical sketch of Harriet Tubman and a poem about her. After reading each one aloud, ask the questions listed at left. Tell students that they are going to think about these questions when planning a new piece of writing.

Using the Overhead Transparency

1. Display the overhead transparency and discuss the headings with students. Explain that "Role" refers to the writer's perspective, "Audience" refers to the intended readers, "Format" describes the form of the writing, and "Topic and Strong Verb" tell about the subject of the piece and the writer's action.

2. Model how to use the graphic organizer. Tell students that you plan to write about a topic such as the renovation of the school cafeteria. Say, "I'll write it as a news story, so I'll write 'news article' under Format. I'll be a reporter, so I'll put that under Role. My audience will be the older kids at this school, so I'll write 'third, fourth, and fifth graders at Clinton Elementary' under Audience. In the last column, I'll write my topic as well as my action: '*teaching* students about the renovation process.'"

3. Ask: "What if I were to change the format and make this into a poem about the renovation?" Cross out your original entries and write "poem" under Format. Then ask students to develop possibilities for the other categories. For instance, you might write from the perspective of a table that's been there for years.

4. Distribute copies of the reproducible and have students use it to plan a new piece of writing.

Taking It Further

Have students record their independent reading selections on a R.A.F.T. graphic. This will encourage them to think about the writer's intended audience and main idea, and help them distinguish between genres.

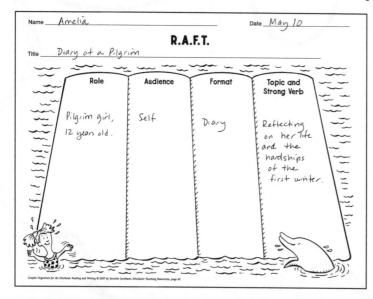

Name Amelia   Date May 10

R.A.F.T.

Title Diary of a Pilgrim

Role	Audience	Format	Topic and Strong Verb
Pilgrim girl, 12 years old.	Self	Diary	Reflecting on her life and the hardships of the first winter.

Graphic Organizers for the Overhead: Reading and Writing © 2007 by Jennifer Jacobson, Scholastic Teaching Resources, page 45

Name _____

Date _____

R.A.F.T.

Title _____

Role	Audience	Format	Topic and Strong Verb

Five W's Star

Purpose

This graphic organizer helps students focus on important information in a story or article. It can provide a structure for students to write summaries of material they have read. They might also use it to help them plan or revise their own nonfiction pieces.

Introducing the Activity

Read aloud a brief newspaper article of local interest. Tell students that they will use a graphic organizer to select and organize the facts essential to this article.

Using the Overhead Transparency

1. Display the overhead transparency. Write the article headline in the center of the star. Ask a volunteer to read the five questions written on the star: Who? What? Why? When? and Where?

2. Ask additional volunteers to provide brief answers to each of the questions. Record their answers under the questions.

3. Distribute copies of the reproducible for students to use with other texts or to plan their own piece of nonfiction writing, such as a newspaper article.

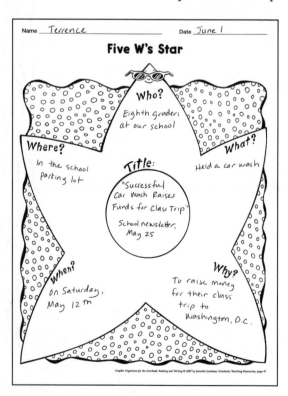

Taking It Further

▶ Ask students to use the graphic organizer when planning an article or story. Explain that the star has limited space and therefore will accommodate only brief notes. Once the planning has been completed, have students expand upon the basic structure in sentence and paragraph form.

▶ Provide students with the graphic organizer to help them determine which information to include when writing a summary. Ask them to think critically about the details they will choose, including only those that answer the five basic questions.

Name _____   Date _____

Five W's Star

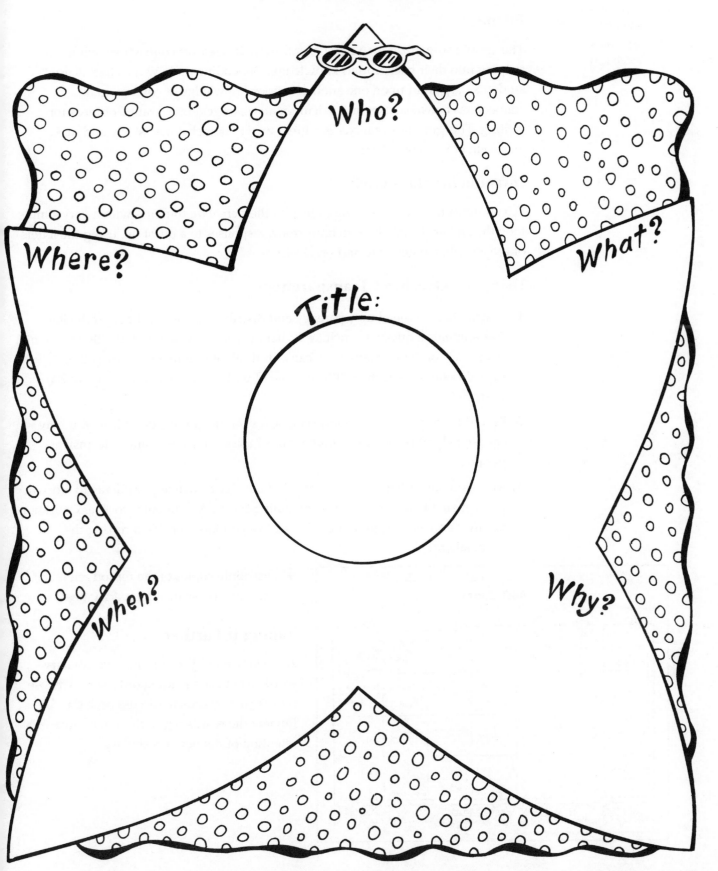

Who?

Where?

What?

Title:

When?

Why?

ABC Chart

Purpose

This graphic organizer inspires students to make creative connections while tapping into their background knowledge. Depending on how the chart is used, students may build upon one another's prior knowledge of content, make connections between texts or curriculum areas, or generate a range of ideas for writing. This graphic organizer is a great way to launch a new study and makes an excellent reference chart.

Introducing the Activity

Tell students that you are going to inspire their creative thinking with a very simple tool: the alphabet. Ask them to brainstorm responses to a question, using the letters of the alphabet to generate and organize ideas.

Using the Overhead Transparency

1. Display the overhead transparency and distribute copies of the reproducible. Ask students a question, such as "What do you know about daily life in Colonial America?" or "How many facts can you think of that relate to desert life?" Provide examples such as "I'll start us off with *s*. 'Some *saguaro* cacti are 200 years old.'"

2. Record responses in the appropriate boxes on the graphic organizer. You may choose to limit responses to one per box or you may allow multiple answers per box.

3. After you have filled in about a third of the chart, challenge students to work in pairs or small groups to fill the remaining boxes. As students work, ask questions to direct and expand thinking, such as "What tools were used during the Colonial era?"

4. Distribute copies of the reproducible for students to use in similar activities.

Taking It Further

As a class activity, record new vocabulary words from class reading or lessons. Choose two or three words to discuss each day. Review the words regularly to reinforce retention of the new vocabulary.

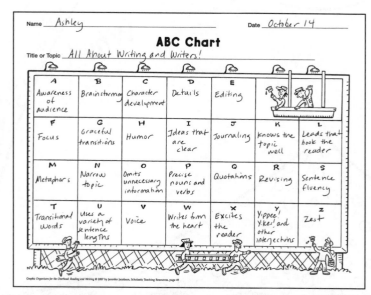

ABC Chart

A	B	C	D	E		
F	G	H	I	J	K	L
M	N	O	P	Q	R	S
T	U	V	W	X	Y	Z

Flexible Use

• Identifying
Cause and Effect
in Literature

• Planning Ideas
for Writing

Cause-and-Effect Crab

Purpose

Identifying cause-and-effect relationships in a story helps students move beyond a literal understanding of the plot. This graphic organizer helps them consider not only what happened in the story but also why it happened. It demonstrates that one cause can have multiple effects, a concept that supports students' understanding of historical relationships, current events, and the implications of personal decisions.

Introducing the Activity

Point out that every decision we make or action we take has consequences, and that these decisions and actions change the course of events. Explain that in the following activity, you will examine the effects of an event in a piece of literature.

Using the Overhead Transparency

1. From a book that you are reading as a class, select an event that has a variety of consequences on the characters and events.

2. Display the overhead transparency and write the pivotal event on the body of the crab under "Cause."

3. Ask students to brainstorm all the consequences of this event, and record their responses on the legs of the crab. Encourage students to consider both the intended and unintended effects of the cause you are discussing.

4. Provide students with copies of the reproducible to use with other events in the same text or with different texts. Or have students use the graphic organizer to plan events and outcomes in their own story writing.

Taking It Further

Suggest that students use the graphic organizer to help them plan a persuasive essay. Have them write the action they hope to bring about in the center of the crab (such as no homework on the weekends), and all the positive benefits of the action in the legs (such as students having more time to read books of their own choosing).

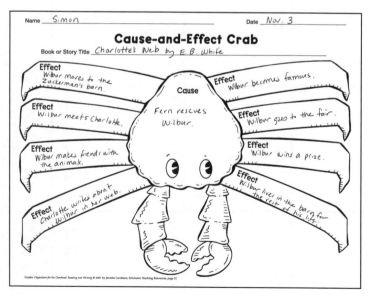

Name _Simon_   Date _Nov. 3_
Cause-and-Effect Crab
Book or Story Title _Charlotte's Web by E. B. White_

Effect Wilbur moves to the Zuckerman's barn.

Cause Fern rescues Wilbur.

Effect Wilbur becomes famous.

Effect Wilbur meets Charlotte.

Effect Wilbur goes to the fair.

Effect Wilbur makes friends with the animals.

Effect Wilbur wins a prize.

Effect Charlotte writes about Wilbur in her web.

Effect Wilbur lives in the barn for the rest of his life.

Graphic Organizers for the Overhead: Reading and Writing © 2007 by Jennifer Jacobson, Scholastic Teaching Resources, page 51

Cause-and-Effect Crab

Book or Story Title _____

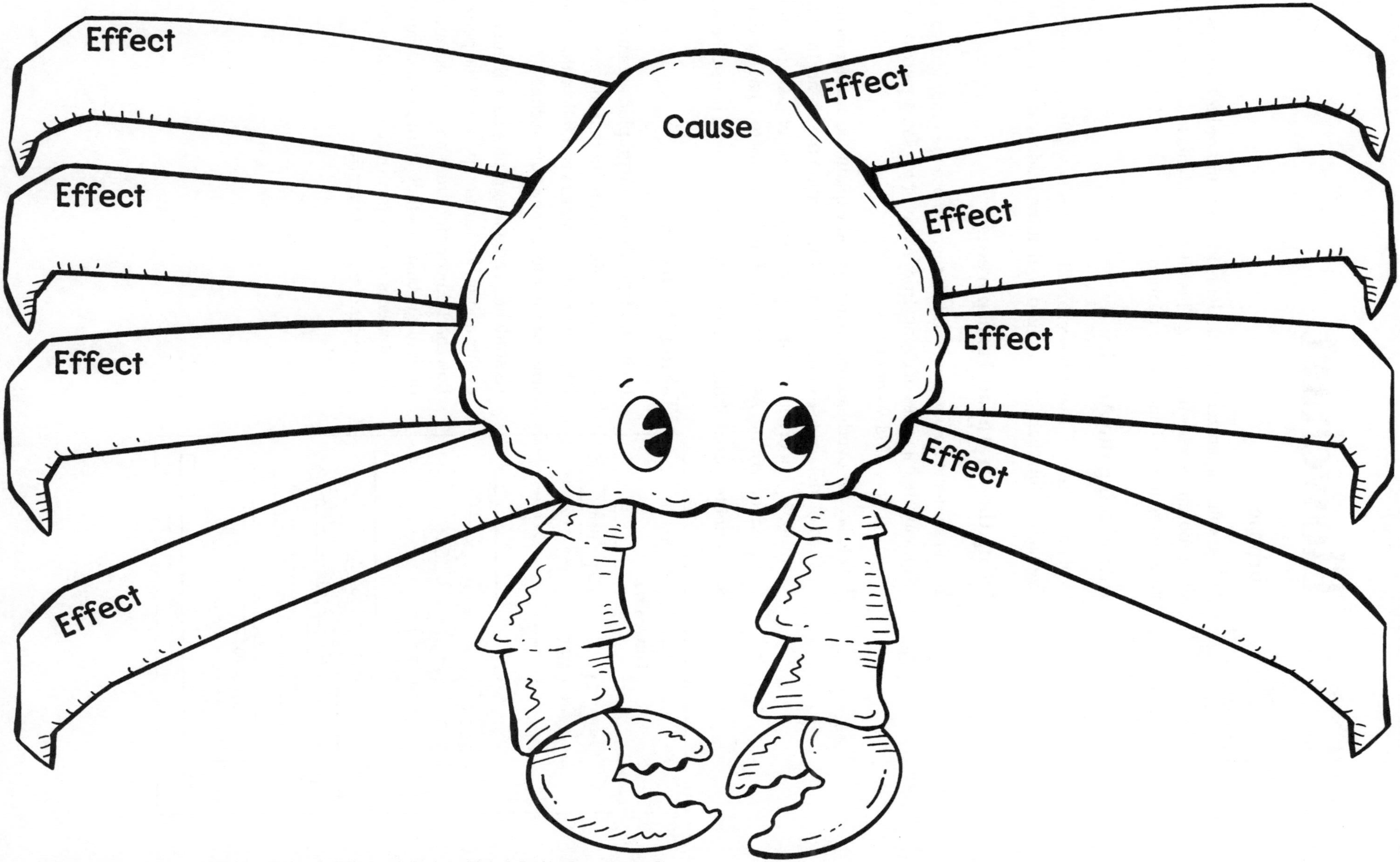

Effect

Effect

Effect

Effect

Cause

Effect

Effect

Effect

Effect

Flexible Use

• Understanding
Sequence
and Causal
Relationships
in Texts

• Organizing
Ideas in Writing

Flowchart

Purpose

This graphic organizer helps students identify and order the steps of a process or the important events in a story. This allows students to understand and distinguish between sequential and causal relationships.

Introducing the Activity

Explain to students that a flowchart illustrates how one event follows another. Events in a flowchart are arranged so that the reader can follow the action logically.

Using the Overhead Transparency

1. Tell students how you would like them to use the graphic organizer: to identify and arrange a series of events from a text or to plan a piece of writing with a logical flow of ideas or events.

2. Display the overhead transparency and explain the arrangement of the flowchart. Then model the use of the chart, either writing the events from a text in chronological order or planning the organization of main points or events for a piece of writing. At the bottom of the chart, write what the diagram shows.

3. Distribute copies of the reproducible for students to use in the way you modeled.

Taking It Further

▶ Invite students to use the graphic organizer when planning a presentation. Remind them that the purpose of the organizer is to ensure that listeners can follow their logic and make sense of their ideas and conclusion.

▶ As students read a biography, have them record significant events and major turning points in the person's life on the flowchart. Encourage students to make more than one draft of the chart; as they learn more about the subject's life, students may come to see the relative importance of particular events differently.

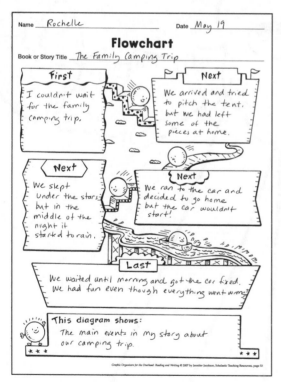

Name _____   Date _____

Flowchart

Book or Story Title _____

First

Next

Next

Next

Last

This diagram shows:

★★★   ★★★

Graphic Organizers for the Overhead: Reading and Writing © 2007 by Jennifer Jacobson, Scholastic Teaching Resources, page 53

Computer Grid

• Comparing
Genre Features

• Structuring an
Author Study

• Evaluating
Writing

Purpose

This graphic organizer helps students build an understanding of a particular genre, an author's work, or a literary element by comparing one work to another. In developing criteria for comparison and testing their theories, students think critically while tapping into and sharing background knowledge.

Introducing the Activity

Show students a simple bar graph or chart and guide them to observe what is being compared and described. Explain how to read the chart or graph and how the axes are labeled. Explain that as a class, you will design a graph that tells about a particular genre (or other subject).

Using the Overhead Transparency

1. Determine how you will use the graphic organizer. Display the overhead transparency and point out that the axes are unlabeled. Ask a question, such as "What are the characteristics of fairy tales?" or "What makes Roald Dahl's books unique?"

2. Record students' answers across the top of the chart, and explain that these are the criteria you will use to compare several works. Ask students to list three titles to compare, and record these along the left side of the chart.

3. Select one title and ask students to decide how each criterion applies, for example: "We said that in Roald Dahl's books, children are often separated from their parents and living with unpleasant relatives. Is that true of Charlie in *Charlie and the Chocolate Factory*?" Develop simple symbols such as "+" or "–" to fill in the boxes on the chart.

* **TIP** *

You might find it useful to add symbols such as S for "sometimes" or "?" for "We're not sure."

4. Distribute copies of the reproducible for students to use in a similar way. Allow time for students to share their work with the class or in small groups.

Taking It Further

Instruct students to use the graphic organizer to evaluate their own writing. Have them write the titles of their pieces down the left side of the chart and the criteria or writing traits across the top.

| Name Howard | | Date May 3 |

Computer Grid

Topic Comparing Fairy Tales

	Begins with "Once upon a time."	Some characters are animals.	Has an antagonist.	Has a happy ending.
Little Red Riding Hood	✓	✓	✓	✓
Cinderella	✓	✓	✓	✓
Three Little Pigs	✓	✓	✓	✓

Computer Grid

Topic _____

• Analyzing the
  Structure of
  Nonfiction
  Writing

• Organizing
  Nonfiction
  Writing

Pinwheel Organizer

Purpose

Expository texts such as persuasive essays or articles often contain a predictable structure: a main idea followed by three major points and supporting details. This graphic organizer helps students identify or analyze the structure and content of expository pieces.

Introducing the Activity

Explain to students that certain kinds of writing revolve around expressing and supporting a central idea. All the details and information in an essay or article are related to the author's main idea or message. Tell students that today's graphic organizer is designed in the shape of a pinwheel, which—like an essay—revolves around a central point.

Using the Overhead Transparency

1. Distribute copies of an essay or article and read it aloud.

2. Display the overhead transparency. Discuss the main idea of the text and write it in the center of the pinwheel.

3. Explain that the author supported this idea with both major supporting points and details. Guide students to identify these points and details, and fill in the rest of the graphic organizer. Point out that the shapes in the pinwheel are symmetrical, and that the supporting points should have equal "weight."

4. Distribute copies of the reproducible to students to analyze nonfiction texts or plan their own.

Taking It Further

Have students use the graphic organizer to plan a three-paragraph essay about a favorite author. Suggest that they write the author's name in the center of the pinwheel. Have them record three major points regarding the author's style, along with detailed examples from different texts. You might also have them use the graphic organizer to plan persuasive essays.

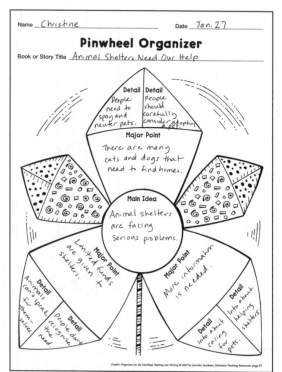

Name _____   Date _____

Pinwheel Organizer

Book or Story Title _____

Detail   Detail

Major Point

Main Idea

Major Point

Major Point

Detail

Detail

Detail

Detail

Graphic Organizers for the Overhead: Reading and Writing © 2007 by Jennifer Jacobson, Scholastic Teaching Resources, page 57

Roller Coaster Story Map

Purpose

This activity introduces students to classic story structure. The graphic organizer can be used as a tool for analyzing literature or for planning and revising stories.

Introducing the Activity

Discuss the idea that stories typically follow a particular path in order to keep a reader oriented and engaged. Most commonly, stories include an introductory section where we come to know the characters and setting; a middle section that includes a problem, obstacle, or change; a climax, where there is great tension, crisis, or transformation; and a resolution, in which the author reveals a message or purpose and leads us out of the story.

Using the Overhead Transparency

1. Choose a familiar fairy tale or other story to illustrate the parts of a story as described above.

2. Display the overhead transparency and point out the placement of the story's climax—the highest point on the roller coaster. Ask students to identify the parts of the sample story and work together to label the roller coaster cars.

3. Distribute copies of the reproducible for students to use with other texts or to plan their own stories.

Taking It Further

▶ Have students use the graphic organizer to prepare for a written book report about their independent reading. Instruct them to use the organizer to help them determine what basic information to include in their report.

▶ Invite small groups to use the organizer to prepare a skit or other dramatic performance. Remind students to use the roller coaster model to help make sure their audience will understand the main parts of the story they are portraying.

Name _____

Date _____

Roller Coaster Story Map

Book or Story Title _____

Resolution

Climax

Middle

Beginning

• Understanding
  Setting in
  Literature

• Constructing
  Settings in
  Writing

Setting Details

Purpose

Authors construct the setting of a story in the mind of the reader through the use of descriptive detail. This graphic organizer helps students develop a vivid image of a book's setting. Students can also use the organizer to help them create a strong setting in their own stories.

Introducing the Activity

Tell students that they will be investigating how authors create vivid, memorable images in the minds of readers: which details they choose to describe, how language can set an overall tone or mood, and how some information can be implied rather than stated explicitly.

Using the Overhead Transparency

1. Distribute copies of a text and ask students to describe a particular setting. Have them search for specific words, phrases, or passages that the author used to create the setting. Provide them with small sticky notes to flag the examples they find.

2. Display the overhead transparency. Ask students to guide you in drawing a sketch of the setting they described. What landscape features or important objects should be included? How can you portray the mood of the setting through color or other details?

3. As you add particular details to your sketch, have students point out the passage from the text that provides this information. Write these details at the bottom of the graphic organizer with the page numbers.

4. Distribute copies of the reproducible. Have students describe and draw a different setting from a text or plan or revise a setting for their own story.

Taking It Further

Read aloud to students the first chapter of a book, and then ask them to use the graphic organizer to draw the setting they imagined. On the bottom half of the page, they can jot down words or phrases that inspire their drawings. After the reading, have students compare drawings. Point out the differences. Help students understand that even though readers use the information from the text to help them visualize the setting, they also use their own background knowledge and creativity.

Name _____   Date _____

Setting Details

Book or Story Title _____

Details That Help Create the Setting	Page

Strategy Sun

Purpose

When students review and name the strategies they use to read, write, or spell skillfully, they better retain and integrate those approaches. This graphic organizer reminds students of the range of strategies at their disposal.

Introducing the Activity

After students have spent time practicing a set of reading, writing, or spelling strategies, ask them to reflect on these techniques. For example, say, "Once you have chosen a topic for a poem, how do you begin to write?" or "When you encounter a word you can't read automatically, what do you do?" Tell students that they will use a graphic organizer to keep track of these ideas.

Using the Overhead Transparency

1. Display the overhead transparency and write the central task (writing a poem, reading an informational text, reading an unfamiliar word, and so on) in the center.

2. Ask volunteers to offer strategies and examples of the strategies in action. Record the strategies on the graphic organizer.

3. Distribute copies of the reproducible and ask students to fill in the remainder of the organizer. Use the graphic organizer throughout the year to review strategies students have learned.

Taking It Further

▶ Have students keep track of new strategies as they are introduced in class. At the end of a unit, they will have collected a list of strategies that they can save in their reading or writing folders for future reference.

▶ Once students have brainstormed strategies, divide the class into pairs or small groups to create posters that will remind students of effective strategies. Display the posters around your classroom.

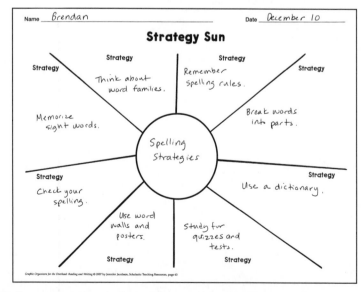

Name _____

Date _____

Strategy Sun

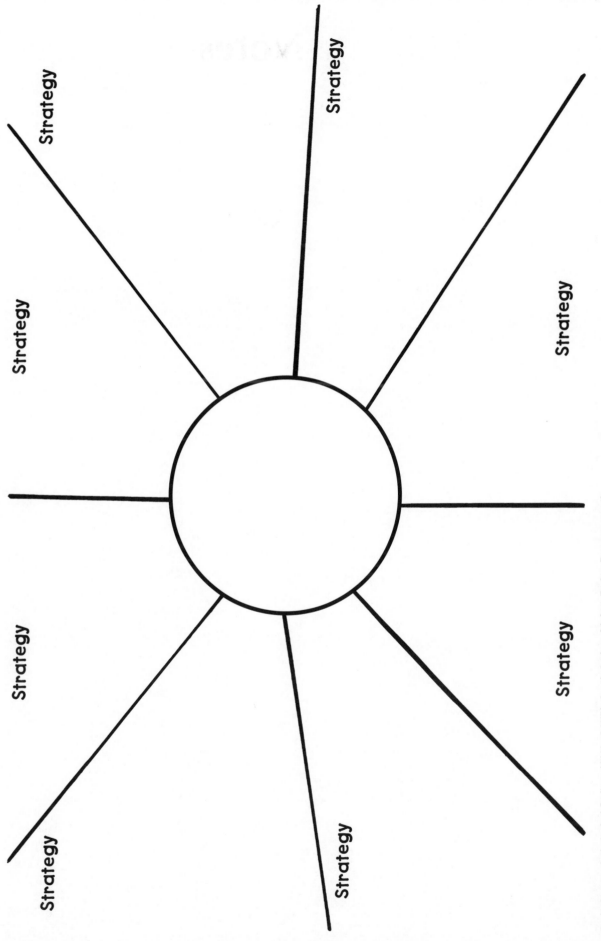

Strategy

Strategy

Strategy

Strategy

Strategy

Strategy

Strategy

Strategy

Notes